They Stand Up In Broken Shells

Poems by Nita Penfold

Cover Art © 1995 Kendrick Wronski, "Planting the Seeds."
Used with permission. www.kendrickwronski.org

Acknowledgments
Some of these poems originally appeared in following:

Mile-High Blue-Sky Pie Chapbook
    (Pudding House Publications, 2002)
Anthologies:
Bless This Child (Skinner House, 2006)
For All That Is Our Life (Skinner House, 2005)
Woman Prayers (HarperSanFrancisco, 2003)
Wedding Blessings (Broadway Books, 2003)
Fresh Water: Poems from the Rivers, Lakes, and Streams
    (Pudding House Publications, 2002)
Mothers and Daughters (Harmony Books, 2001)
Split Verse (Midmarch Arts Press,2000)
Family Celebrations (Andrew McKeel Publishing, 1999)
At Our Core (Papier Mache Press, 1998)
Prayers to Protest: Poems That Center and Bless Us (Pudding
    House Publications, 1998)
Claiming the Spirit Within (Beacon Press, 1996)
Women and Death (Ground Torpedo Press, 1994)
Writing Our Way Out of the Dark (Queen of Swords Press, 1995)

Magazines: The New Yorker, (Talk of the Town Review of Split
Verse, July 10, 2000), Sojourner, Coming of Age, Earth's
Daughters , Slipstream, The Maryland Poetry Review, Sublime
Odyssey, Common Ground, Poetry Motel, Up Against the Wall,
Mother; Blueline, Lactuca, Pacific Coast Journal, Edicion
Feminista, Imagine, Art Centering, Exit 13, Barefoot Grass
Journal, Buffalo News, Pudding Magazine, Kumquat Meringue,
Aurorean, The Haven, New Poetry.

Table of Contents

3 We Are Born Again

They Stand Up In Broken Shells

Calling

CALLING

You wake to the honey
light before anyone else, perch
on the long wooden stairtop,
wishing to be old enough to
drag the wide-bottomed boat
out alone, to command the creak
of oars, the water's flash, to
steer to where the Buddha-frogs
nightly chant their steely croak,
where the water spiders stride
across the surface like complacent
miracles, where something calls
to you like the red-winged blackbird
clinging to the high reeds skirting
the lake and you want to purse
your mouth just so
and answer,   *yes,*
yes.

THAT SUMMER, OPEN

She likes herself at Grandma's.
Paint peels off in strips from the door,
smooth black china knob wiggles in her hand
then opens to the summer sky hot
on her freckled tan, legs eight summers long.
Best strawberry picker around,
she doesn't eat any, but carefully pushes apart
hairy leaves, choosing only the rich red bumpy ones.

On the field's edge, a killdeer runs
screaming away from her, wing flopping.
Grandma shows her the eggs like round
speckled rocks careless in the dirt.
The day they hatch, the baby birds are fluffy,
they stand up in broken shells and then all run away.

BIRTHDAY PHONE CALL
FROM MY GRANDMOTHER

She tells the story, as she does every year,
about the night that I was born,
when she hurried to stay with my brother.
How the worst blizzard in seven years
covered everything with rough cotton batting,
earth and sky playing deadly hide-and-seek.
The road disappeared under white bullets
driven against the windshield
forcing her car into the field.
How she struggled on foot, chill sting
biting into her face, tearing through her thin coat.
She fought the wind for short shallow breaths
How the two yellow eyes traveling toward her
like a sci-fi vision, turned into the county plow.
She flagged it down and rode, up in the high cab,
                                        to the house.

Her warm voice crackles over the phone wire:
What a night that was, so many years ago now,
I'll never forget it, that night you were born.
You were close to coming before I got there!
I can almost see her large frame sitting
at the shiny Formica-topped table,
holding the phone in loose-skinned hands;
green eyes like round glass beads,
hair, sheared lamb's wool. The kitchen smells
of ancient linoleum-and-grease.
Her apron-print dress sticks to the plastic chair
as she huddles near the hot stove, chuckling.

IF I WERE TO BELIEVE IN A MALE GOD

If I were to believe in a male God
He'd resemble my father: gray whiskers
grow sideways when He forgets they need trimming;
white hair curls to His thick neck in waves
so perfect I suspect setting lotion, hair clips;
above His ears, the edges try to take off
into horns, but He combs them down carefully.
The top of His head's a speckled egg, shiny,
freckled, with a few struggling survivors
left of the lush growth in old black
& white photographs of Him as a young man.

Like my father, God comes home
from his suit-and-tie speeches and His desk,
changes into worn jeans with a flannel shirt,
climbs the steep ladder and repairs the shingled roof.
Weekends, He knocks out walls and adds windows,
tinkers with lawn mower engines, refrigerator valves,
fixes clogged drains, recalcitrant ovens,
raises toasters from the dead. Neighbors stop by,
His children call long-distance for help
to change the washing machine belt,
or ask if He's got an extra television handy.

Above all, God would have to be a benevolent monarch,
all bluster; stomach a little large for His tall frame,
an overfondness for lemon meringue pie
and stolen spoonsful of Heavenly Hash.
Brown eyes twinkle as He provokes arguments
for their own sake. He chuckles over our little
disagreements, blushes over our indiscretions,
but would forgive us anything
to have all His children home eating at His table again.

AT THIRTEEN, I UNDERSTOOD
WHAT LOVE WAS ALL ABOUT

Not all those groping scenes from movie ads
rated X by the Legion of Decency, nor
the quick dry kisses in closets
during furtive spin-the-bottle games, nothing
to do with the lean bodies of boys
hanging out the bus windows--whistling, nor
the envious computation of bra sizes
in the girls' locker-room.

Perching on the bed's edge next to Grandpa
one week after Grandma died,
I watched the thin stripes of light
between tight-shut blinds
glowing across Grandpa's bent back.
This sackman, loosely stuffed into white shirt,
bow tie, thin suspenders, dark baggy pants,
little hairs standing out like thorns
against his pale skin—where was the
dapper change-jingler, the bald cigar-puffer?
Withdrawn.

                                    In the stillness,
I felt a shifting, the mesh shredding,
rending the fifty-year weave of six children, a barn,
some pigs, Christmas Eve poker games.
Grandpa rested his hand on mine and sighed
in an anguish that prickled up and down my spine;
I can't go on without her.
And, when he died so soon after—
I realized I'd seen eternal love,
and started in search of my own.

THE KISS

Pressed against
twin blossoms
Sweet lilacs blooming
I am drunk with bliss

COMING TO KNOW YOU IS LIKE

walking up out of the basement coffee shop
on a summer's night in Harvard Square and
cutting through a quiet side street as I've
done a thousand times; stopping short
as an elephant wearing a red fez and perched
on a broad cylinder raises his two front legs
in a delicate dance step, surrounded by women
in fancy cocktail dresses shimmering in
the streetlight and men in elegant tuxedos
who all hold champagne glasses.

Wonder tumbles me backward in time:
was I eight or ten when the stubbled field
up the street grew tents that flopped
in the wind, squirty clowns cavorting in
sawdust, glittery trapeze artists flinging
themselves high toward each other
while we held our breath; and
an elephant so close I touched
the rough gray bags of hairy skin—
as if a wrinkled suit made too big so that
someday it would surely grow into it;
larger than real life, magic
that one misty morning vanished,
only evidence left, popcorn bags caught
still in the spiky weeds and a circle of
sawdust the wind slowly wiped away.

BLOOD DRAW

The pull of blood monthly
draws me into images
of invisible suckling babes;
soft round buttocks,
sweet shimmering eyes
helplessly floating within;
my body compels me
to send my seed
into warm communion with his;
fulfillment comes though a heavy belly,
ripe for the delivery
of a long-forgotten maternal promise.

And only reluctantly
do I refuse.

CERAMIC FROM A CATHOLIC KITCHEN

The Madonna of the Kitchen stands serene
in her white robe, blue mantle modestly covering
her bowed head. Face porcelain, empty, eyes closed.
Behind her golden halo the cupboards are neatly
lined with crockery. She is barefoot, and holds
a fresh loaf of bread on a white cloth with her left hand.
With her right, she touches lightly the curly blonde head
of a small barefoot child, angelic, who
reaches on tiptoe to touch her.

This Madonna is never angry at the child, who would
never fingerpaint with yogurt on the linoleum floor.
There are no raspberry jam splotches
on the refrigerator like grand Picasso forms.
No dried peanut butter on the table leg,
no spilled Cheerios crushed to a fine dust underfoot,
no chili plastered on the wall behind the highchair.
This house does not smell like a subway entrance.
The child never tries to flush the washcloth down
the toilet. The sink is not lost under two days of
encrusted dishes; nor is the table piled with a jumble
of socks, sweatshirts, towels, and training pants
waiting impatiently to be folded.

This Madonna will never be found, crouched
at the crack in the bathroom door, trying
to keep her laughter controlled, as she watches
her daughter pull the tampons one by one from
their cardboard tubes into the warm bathwater
where they swell suddenly, large and white.

ADOLESCENCE

At night while she sleeps
I unravel the rope that binds us;
jute rubs its rough fibers into my skin.
I loosen one strand at a time
picking it apart with torn fingernails.

Watching her in sleep, I remember
that newborn moon-face, dark cornsilk hair;
compact body resting well-molded
to the comfort of my soft belly.
She would awaken, wide eyes surprised
at the distance traveled from protective waters.

In the morning, she takes her stance.
We are eye-to-eye, rope to rope, a tug of war.
Her newly-breasted body stands stiffly away.
She throws her whole weight from me,
every muscle anticipating flight—
from the shackles she sees me hold
from the darkness that passes unspoken between us.

Once I was where she now stands, struggling against
the bond, pulling away from the mirror
in my mother's eyes, sweat clouding my sight.
Now I tug at my child less and less, terrified
she might end sprawling in the mud, afraid
of her reflex hatred, that coiled mistrust of freedom.

Fierce, proud of each inch of victory,
she seeks what I am only now finding
hopes for answers she thinks I can give.
I let the rope go slack a little at a time,
and take courage from her triumphant face.

THIS IS A POEM

This is a poem

This is a poem for

This is a poem for Mrs. C.
whose face I cannot remember

This is a poem for Mrs. C.
whose long hands had brown/ink/spots

This is a poem for Mrs. C.
whose blue/veined/scratched fingers
passed out the paper, one sheet to a child

This is a poem for Mrs. C., *NO MISTAKES NOW*
who watched over my skinny shoulder
as I fumbled to pencil the apple and banana
propped on Sister Alicia's desk

This is a poem for Mrs. C. who clicked her tongue
against the roof of her mouth and shook her head
until the fluorescent lights seemed to flicker & fade

This is a poem for Mrs. C. who clicked her tongue
and pronounced YOU CAN'T DRAW as if that was all
there was to it until the end of time//
and something closed up small inside me

This is a poem for Mrs. C.

This is a poem for

NO

This is a poem

This is a poem for longing

This is a poem for all the longing
locked inside these fingers

This is a poem for the morning glories
I would not draw

This is a poem for the pale pink of dawn reflected
in their fluted mouths, the little trumpets that folded
up into fans on pale stems in the broad light

This is a poem for the strong clean lines
of the tiger lilies

This is a poem for their thick green stalks topped
with an orange so fierce it burned within me

This is a poem

YES

This is a poem

This is a poem for Amy with the paint-soaked rags

This is a poem for Amy at college where
Beginning Art meant that you could already do it

This is a poem for Amy who painted at night
because she couldn't work with all those fish/eyes

staring in the open bowl of studio

This is a poem for Amy who taught me to play
with light & shadow, pen & ink
and who tried to make Mrs. C.'s voice go away

This is a poem for Amy

This is a poem

YES

This is a poem

This is a poem for my daughters
who had crayons and paper before they could walk

This is a poem for my daughters who colored
& cut & ripped & played

This is a poem for my daughters who had oil pastels,
modeling clay, wood, yarn, fabric scraps, egg cartons,
poster paint, chalk, felt-tip markers, and seventeen
different weights and textures of paper culled
from garbage cans and garage sales

This is a poem for my daughter, Sara, who drew
the inside of a chestnut at the age of four

This is a poem for my daughter, Kate, who
drew a book a faces before she was three

This is a poem for my daughters whose teachers
say *YES*, your drawings are good

YES, your lines are clean, your composition fine

This is a poem for my daughters

YES

This is a poem for them

DAUGHTER MINE

Your breasts are smooth vanilla mounds
topped with ripe raspberries,
soon you will grow into blood rites
and the confusion of mixed parts;

your father suspects a conjurer's trick
or scientific accidents induced
by eating injected chickens; poor man,
he is fearful of growing old;

I rejoice in the awakening:
you firmly believe on one hand
that you will never live away from me;
on the other, you are a seeker
who delves into distant deserts
anxious to bring forth waters.

QUESTIONS NEVER ASKED

Why didn't you
tell me, Momma,
about the altar;
legs rising
like marble columns
pink flesh soft between,
worshipped by tongue?
Did you have words, Momma,
for secret chambers
that breathe, moist
bellows filling
in and out
out and in,
waves traveling higher
toward the fire?
The fire, Momma,
have you touched the fire?
Majestic warmth
grounding center,
electric storm-laden lightning
that flings against the eyelids
to fly outward
singing.

AS I WATCH MY DAUGHTER MARRY

I remember her at eleven:
she will not let me love her,
slams the door between us,
wants to be grown so fast but
complains as her nipples widen,
soft and tender and aching.
I wish I could explain to her how
fast everything goes by and that I need
to slow it all down, but she is always
pushing for something more that she
imagines is a prize for being older and
we can never come to agreement over terms.

In a calm moment on her grandmother's back porch,
we discover an infant robin who flew too early
on the lawn under the box elder, bottom-heavy
like a diapered baby, its stick wings
working furiously, barely lifting it back up
toward its rough nest again and again.
Both of us afraid to touch the bird for fear
its mother might abandon it from our scent,
we watch the baby's struggle, cheering it on,
and my daughter slides
closer to me on the step.

IN MY WILD IMAGININGS:

because of my deep darkness
I have always known my heart capable
of this true centering, this capacity for
strong longing, for impassioned joy
as if a horde of butterflies are rising
through me to float in the bright midsummer air.
There is no measuring cup broad enough
to hold this love, no container
that will enclose it without
busting its sides; there are no
edges to it, no bottom, no top;
wider than any logical ruler
could figure, taller than any tape
marked off in consistent inches,
or feet or yards; no odometer
can track the distance it travels to you
without time, within such boundless space.
It is so beyond rational knowing and into
the realm of be-ing, bursting through
the seams of my small heart like
fairy lights shimmering upon the wild ocean waves.

IN MY GRANDDAUGHTER'S EYES

I do not own the language of my granddaughter
but I see the spark, that luminous wisdom
shining from her intense blue eyes.
In awe, I watched her labor into this world
in concert with, and out of, my daughter's body.
Now she grasps at my forefinger,
moves her pale eyebrows, purses those thin lips
struggling to speak, her knowledge ancient
and translucent as her newborn skin.
I try to reach through the layers between us,
touch the shape of this wisdom
that comes with us all, something we lose
when we grow to learn the language of this world,
something we are always searching for
to make our lives whole once again.
Her spirit is not familiar with her small body,
kicks and thrashes to test the limits of this new being.
I hear her singing, *I am here,*
it is life again, saying yes to the universe,
yes with absolute delight and sorrow.
Be here now, I hear her implore,
in my eyes is the universe.
Look. Feel it once again. Sing with me.

MID-JUNE ECSTASY

Sea colored green-mottled marble,
white caps urgent in their chase to the shore,
wind a cool buttress buoying the gull's silent wings.
Black-bibbed sparrows rut on the boulders
rising above the faded females in a frenzy; two
bikes lie abandoned on the seawall, the boy and girl
down at the edge of the swirl pulling tangled kelp
from mussel shells split open like erect angel's wings.

How the sun heats this wintered skin,
how the wind engulfs me with its fecund breath,
how the day chides we who can see nothing larger
than ourselves in the bluebell sky, in the smallest
crusty starfish, in the speckled rocks. Sometimes I
feel I will burst with this beauty, this spirit.
Oh, what a paltry word, god.

SHE SPEAKS

I am as young, as new
as the seed between two
held in rapture
split with wanting

I am as old as rock,
as enduring as a minute,
as solid as
a butterfly's wing

I am the young birch sapling
bent so far in the wind
its branches grow
into roots

Begin

BEGIN

"You must begin with 'I cannot tell'"
--Muriel Rukeyser

I cannot tell how grief
hollowed a child's body out
and made a woman's shell.

I cannot tell how death slid
into a small life and opened it
suddenly, like a door with a cold draught.

I cannot tell about the voice that calls me
in my sleep, that tiny fat woman who carefully
sews together the lips of children

with black thread;
they are already silent,
it is only a precaution.

I cannot tell.

CATHOLIC CHILD

Forced to sit during recess
I guarded the votive candles like my faith,
feared someone would break

into the darkened church
and light one without
proper payment to God.

Whispers echoed hollow
in heavy emptiness,
rituals hung crucified

against great gothic walls;
it was hard to breathe
in the cramped shallow

of rubbed oak pews.
Church too still
to hold a god, too small.

Stained glass distorted
light into fragments and shapes
that held no pattern for me;

I longed for wide sky
broken by the pleading arms of trees,
open horizon line

still not vast enough to hold
the wellings of wonder
which served as my prayers.

SALVATION

Some days the girl saved her pennies
for fluorescent statues of the Virgin Mary
with lowered eyes, holding the chubby Babe.
She left the figure on the windowsill
to soak up the sun. By night, Mary's face shone,
like her mother's in the eerie light of the tv:
tired and sad. The child longed to stroke
those lines away from the eyes, out of the forehead;
but her hands only fidgeted in her lap,
shredding the skin around her fingernails.
Later, she rubbed the glowing green statue
against her face to soothe herself to sleep.

Other days, she gave her pennies for the pagan babies,
fat-bellied with stick-bone legs. Their pictures
were tacked to the bulletin board at school.
Wide eyes dark chocolate pools:
mirrors without reflection.
They sucked at the brown breast-bags dazed,
flies crawling across eyelids, clinging to lips.
Their mothers were wrapped tightly in old rags,
faces worn to that same sorrow as her mother's.
The girl wanted them to be saved, as she was,
dipped into cool waters, cleansed and fed,
clothed in God's light.
But, mostly, she just wanted them all to smile.

LETTER TO MY OLDER BROTHER
CONCERNING THE CATHOLIC CHURCH

You ask me why I am so angry about exclusion
and all-male priesthoods. Remember when
we were children, I helped you build
the treehouse on the edge between field and woods;
yanked squealing nails from old planks,
lugged heavy two-by-fours, ignored splinters
from rough boards sawed the way you told me to?

When the platform was finished,
you wouldn't let me in--
pushed me out until I went home wailing.
Oh, I could worship there when you were gone,
leaving my offerings spread out for the birds.
The sweetness of hay filled the air.
I loved the ribbed bark against my back,
suggestion of possibility in the endless sky.
But you always found me and I stomped away,
kicking at the innocent grass, confused
by my so-called sins against your sanctuary.

After a time, you went on to bigger trees
in the deep woods, where I wasn't allowed
because "things happened to little girls" there.
I got your hand-me-down house, hard-fought-for,
no victory came with it,
no quieting my hunger for unnamable things;
in this, too, I made do with what I was left.

I will
make do
no longer.

FAULT LINES

I know the chasm that comes
upon the soul, wearied;
it snaps back your hand
into a child's face--
the feeling shames me
and I drive myself into bathrooms
and closets to hold my breath.
I know the crack,
the rift the earthquake leaves
that sucks you in;
you grab at anything
to avoid that black plunge,
even hurling words
that can break against a child's skull.
I know how the young ones die;
I fear
the clenching of my fists
into hard white knobs
that cannot belong to me.
The newspaper haunts with stills
of fresh faces lost
since the last newscast;
I shake my fist at the screen
and crumple the paper,
hugging my children near.

I AM SEARCHING FOR THE EDGES OF THINGS TO HOLD ONTO:

the 90 degree angle of the laminated
table slippery, resisting touch;
bookcase's metal corner sharp,
feral, with ornamental jaws.
When this mad passion sweeps in, a wave
tumbling over me, I want to fling myself
against something hard, a brick wall,
prickly pine needles, dead leaves that
crackle to dust in my hands. Something wants
to tear loose in me, and when it releases,
I fear I will drown from lack of touch.

These are days of awful emptiness. I reach
inside and there is nothing, nothing there
but an echo that resounds until
I sleep within its repetition.
I am uneasy with softness.
Pillows have no edges, just go on and on
in a siege of comfort that smothers my heart.

ROLLING STONES

Pebble people come rolling
      from their houses each day,
            gathering no moss, no moss.

Life's etchings on their faces
      are flames of forgotten fans
            spreading in milk/white

paper/gray and tortoise/tooled lines,
      gathering no moss, no moss.
            Worn smooth by sharp tumbles,

they confuse faster and faster
      spilling slick pieces to the sidewalk
            from the zippers the hospital never closed,

gathering no moss, no moss.
      Doubled shopping bags clutched--
            thick skins to collect the lost,

threadbare bones misplaced
      skin bleached smooth
            scarecrow eyes loosely staring.

Stuffing them back
      disarranged, the pebble people
            pull close, protective

gathering no moss, no moss.

THERE IS NO POETRY IN DYING:

the stomach's upheaval
numbing hands and feet
confusion spreading across your face
followed by frustration,
your hand stroking mine,
grateful for small miracles:
the weather turning warm,
a visiting baby's smile,
old photographs, finding
the children's story
you abandoned years ago.

Making plans is impossible;
it is only moment to moment
you can be sure of,
and even that is a thread.
A home health aide says all the brain
cancer patients die in their sleep.
You must already know, trying to stay
awake as late into the night as possible
watching funny movies one after another.

I bring you
Uncle Willy's DEATH BY CHOCOLATE,
the immortal dessert sauce from New England,
and we joke: if you've got to go,
do it with chocolate. Death is an adventure, you say,
thanking me for companioning your journey
but what I feel is guilt for not quitting
my job, being with you until the end.

There is no poetry in your dying
yet I try to shape it into something
smooth that I can handle
like the cool violet amethyst you give me
that I worry back and forth between my fingers
as I listen to your rattling breath,
helping you to hold on for news
of your coming grandchild,
you helping me to let go.

CONVERSATION WITH GOD OVER
FETTUCINE IN THE NORTH END, BOSTON

I don't believe in you.

He nods, shaking parmesan cheese over his pasta,
swirling it up onto his fork neatly. Dark wood glows
with muted stained-glass colors from
the Tiffany lamps above.

I don't believe in you because you cannot exist.

He beckons the waiter to pour more wine,
smacking his broad lips as he sips it.
Tall, elegant in gray wool, his slightly-long white hair
brushed away from dark amused eyes. I squirm against
the tight-packed tables avoiding the brush of his knees.

*I cannot take seriously all those trappings: miracles,
virgin birth, resurrection, old stories.*

Suddenly, a tenor voice sings seductively in my ear.
I blush; my eyes are caught by the braided garlic tangled
with dusty rubber grapes on the wall beside him.
He sops up the rest of the clam sauce
with a piece of torn bread, twirling it soggily
around on the gold-rimmed plate.

I don't believe in you.

He pats his mouth with a large linen napkin and smiles. Leaning so close as he gets up to leave that I can smell the mixture of Old Spice and Chianti, he whispers,

"Then why do you keep talking to me?"

SMALL TOWN WOMAN

drives with the brakes on
slow, pulling against
the automatic transmission
she worries that she might hit
a tree, might scratch the fender
might crash into a thousand pieces
flying through the air

the pain becomes unbearable
she waits at the railroad crossing
too long
she perfects her timing

SHE IS GOING BACK INTO
HER DARK IMAGES:

this is her body, scarred and flabby
holding the pain inward from childhood,
her mind chanting:

nothing happened
it's all in your imagination
you made it all up.

This is her blood, a drop
glistening crimson down her thigh,
another in a trail on the porcelain tub.

The skinny child within twists
in terror at night now, begging
for protection, reassurance.

All the woman can offer her is
a stuffed lop-eared rabbit, soft and yielding
as she hugs it to her chest.

SUICIDE POEMS

#1
I try to
drown myself
in the bathtub
but
the bubbles
make me
sneeze.

#2
She shows me
the two thin white stripes
on the back of
the deep green needles
that make it hemlock
and I think
do you steep them
like tea,
do you eat them,
how does the poison work?

#3
considering
the absurdity
of flossing
my teeth
while I
think of
ways to kill myself

EPISODE AT BRY-LIN HOSPITAL

she says   she remembers
                      nothing
                            of that time

she stifles
the giggles rising--
bubbles in her throat--
she strangles thoughts
that come from nowhere--
floating loose on a sea of chemicals
cauterized by welding torches

she hoards her screams
(if she gives away too many
they will bind
her arms)

she says   she remembers
                      nothing
                            of that time

except
                  sudden   brilliant   intensity

                              falling OFF

into

                  nothingness

that void frightened her
she couldn't remember

                              WHERE

she was sitting

                              HOW

she came to be

                              WHY

the strangers

she watched the garage
from her window
cars swallowed by walls
aching for something
she couldn't name

she poses
(a mannequin)
hands placed exactly
center in her lap--
face smooth (dead)
then puzzled--

                          who are you?
                          she asks her daughter.

YOUR LOVE IS

a weight I bear;
it is cracking me--
grinding my bones
down to mere meal,
leaving me
a dry heap
on the bare boards.

I am weary
of between lives:
woodwork cracks
where tongue
misses groove, shrunken.
I am wary
of the wind
in your eyes,
your silent
indrawn breath.

WHEN I THINK NOW OF YOU

I see that funny house on our way to the Jersey Shore,
Victorian, rising up severe and straight-edged.
In my memory every floor's a contrasting color,
each one taller and skinnier
than the one below,
the top narrowing
to a square wide enough
to hold only a spindly straight-backed chair,
an artificial story added
to exaggerate the building's height,
like a whimsical throne towering over us
peering up from the pavement below.
But there is no way to reach the chair,
no ladder or window
close enough so that someone
could climb her way up and sit
to survey the rich view it surely offers.
It perches there, alone,
the clouds framing it.

HER DAUGHTER'S FUTURE WEDDING

All she can think about
is being in the same room
as her ex-husband.
The knives on the table.

I AM BORDERING ON THE EDGE OF CHAOS,

its darkness is full of life sleeping.
I go inside myself and shut the door tightly,
then dream of car crashes and train wrecks
where I pull children from the flames.
I think they are my children, but
after the rescue, I do not recognize them.

There are always two, one older girl,
a younger boy. I turn back again and again
to the burning, feeling as if I left
someone behind to die.
Each day I awake covered with stones.

HERE IS THE CHURCH WITH THE RED DOOR

I don't know if the door was always red
but I can see it now from where I stand
on the road next to the cemetery with
my grandfather's grave in the cold snow,
so it is the church with the red door.
Into the church go a little girl and her
grandmother. The little girl likes to play
in the small basement church school rooms with
the tiny chairs and pictures of Jesus while
her grandmother cleans upstairs in the polished
sanctuary, and her grandfather mows the lawn
outside. But the lights go off and her chair
tips over and it is so dark and someone puts
something hard and slimy into her mouth so that
she can't breathe, someone heavy who pushes on
top of her and makes her hurt. She doesn't
understand why this is happening, what is happening,
and a voice whispers that she is a bad girl
and better not tell, that Jesus won't love her anymore
for doing this in his church. And she doesn't
tell because she has no words for what happened, no
pictures from the dark, and after awhile,
it doesn't matter that Jesus no longer loves her,
because she doesn't love herself.

EQUINOX

My mother doubts her healing,
too broken by someone's imagined stare.
But, on the cemetery carpet of wax-brown leaves,
she kneels at the urn on her young son's grave
unconcerned with her appearance—
soil beneath her fingertips, smudge on her ivory skin,
gray curls undone by bittersweet air.
In this act of prayer, she's lost to self—
facial muscles relaxed, totally absorbed
as she re-pots the geraniums for the winter—
picking off the pungent dead blossoms
gently taking velvet leaves
between thumb and forefinger,
washing autumn's dust away
digging up the roots to be bound once more
in this offering: to lie dormant for a season
within porch walls, then replanted in the spring,
its blossoms thinly fluttering in the breeze
like a folded prayerbook, red-rimmed pages
opening again and again.

IN THE HALF-MOON TIME

She drives herself relentlessly,
glutting her body with
moldy seeds, starving
her soul on dreams
half-digested, leaving no time for
the roundness, the richness
of the August night,
peepers burping in the wetness,
crickets hiccupping their raspy
song in the lush bushes;
no time to go deep.

Like the moon being swallowed
by a haze of polluted clouds,
she is disappearing
into forward motion,
trying not to notice
she is really standing still.

IN MY DREAM

I tell my mother that
I didn't make it up, crying
because she doesn't believe me.
My dead brother and I are
in an unknown cement-block shower,
my grandfather watches us
silently behind his pipe,
he wears a red-and-black hunting
jacket and a green cap.

In my dreams, I am continually crippled
in a car accident. I see it happen,
feel the crush of the steel, the snap
of my back, but there is no pain.
Sometimes while crippled, I help a woman
in the back of a narrow taxi to deliver
her twins, one whole and beautiful, the other
horribly deformed. Other times, I hide a baby
under a blanket in the lap of my wheelchair
from the terrorists with machine guns
who sweep into the room, praying
the child will not suffocate.

                              But sometimes
I sit alone in my wheelchair on a high
walkway overlooking the raging sea, the drop
a comfort before me.

IN THE WAITING

My daughter writes a story for English class
in which a woman waits in a dark room, not
eating or sleeping, simply waiting. A sad
story and her teacher marks the pages red,
gives it a low grade, says it should have had
a happy ending, refuses to recognize the truth
in the silence of the waiting woman, in that time
we always find ourselves, the emptiness of
waiting for our real lives to begin, beyond
the mundane tasks, the duties; we wait for school
to end, for our partners, our children, our bosses,
our lovers, our work to be done, but what then?
We wait for our dreams behind closed shutters,
drawn drapes, thinking they will find us if
only we wait long enough. It is an untruth we all hope
will be true. And the dreams die in our waiting
as we sit in hollow rooms, the silence deafening.

STIGMATA

Seven screws make a line down my mother's back,
the eighth has broken off. Wire crisscrosses
through them to hold her rib cage tight;
breathing becomes difficult.
Her neck vertebrae stack together with diaper pins.

I find relics of release before this, some sense
of wanting, of a self unproscribed or at least not
denied—thin faded paper with meticulously corrected
type returned from Reader's Digest, her scuffed
tan bowling shoes borrowed in high school,
thick black 78's of Deanna Durbin.

Then the weight and the limit and the joys of children
(one dead) spiraling into adults, the grandchildren,
great grandchildren, a grand façade erected around her.
Each one pulling her back to assigned roles;
(when did she get to choose?)
each one tightening the wire.

Her heart is breaking.
She has become her own cage.

IN GRANDMOTHER'S GARDEN

The snake curls glistening,
mounds & mounds of black rope
coiled thick on furrowed rows
crushing small green/yellow shoots
that push up through damp soil;
the day is dark, overcast.

In my dream, the day is bright;
I am a small child with long dark hair.
Bursts of color bloom everywhere.
I grab the black snake by its tail:
in my hand it lies thick and dry
and warm. I lift slowly, swing it
into the air above my head.
It glides around & around;
when I let go the snake flies
out of the garden, over the wall
forever. I am dizzy with joy.

My grandmother guides the tractor;
she is a goddess, upright
resolute as she drives over the snake
again & again, cutting it into sections
then plowing it under with the newly
sprouted beans; her short dark hair
a shining crown, the tractor a sword.
She has been to church,
she knows the temptations of
a serpent let loose in the garden.

She begins to plant again.

We Are Born Again

MY POEMS

come to me hard-fisted
with mean mouths
they are not polite ladies
will not be still
they won't stay where I put them
nor keep my secrets.
I like their red-rough hands,
their ready grins
the way they yank and unravel
my bindings, and won't let me sleep
until they let loose my soul.

ROOM CATALOGUE

At the top of the house, up the narrow staircase,
my room perches, a bird ready for flight.
This nest is too full: piles of unread books
stacked like tottering empires, dusty tv unplugged,
an avalanche of poems on the nightstand.
Stiff Egyptian figures crowd the walls, surround
small windows where sun and trees peek in.
The scent of sandlewood drifts from ashes
dead in a bowl; clanking radiator hisses
its hot breath at the single bed buried
under blankets and an old sleeping bag.
On the bureau, a city of vitamin bottles encircles
the glassy smear of spilled tea.

This nest is too empty: my children's faces smile
from glossy photographs taped to the mirror.
Blonde pony-girl with laughing eyes,
her sister dark with risen beauty, trying to grin.
I go to stroke them often, soft as silk,
after long phone conversations in the dark.
I imagine their contours under my hands, their warmth.

On the long polished desk, my typewriter
is shining silver.
It squats in the sun, like a great gray toad
ready to leap at my touch.

KITES FLY, PLASTIC IMITATIONS

of the circling gulls crying
like new nails being pulled
from thick boards. In the graveyard
a kite crashes, three tiers
collapsing. The gulls hang in
the strong wind mocking these
attempts to mirror their effortless
rise and fall, a slight dip in the
wings, a tip of the body and
they are dancing in the blue.

A young girl with one long blonde
braid down her back arranges
the purple, blue and green streamers
in the graveyard, smoothing and
straightening them like a wedding
train or a precious veil caught
in the long grass. When the kite rises
finally, they dance against
the sunset, circling and swirling
like wild writing in the sky.

ON CREATION

Leather bellows blister into the yawn
of fire, forcing this iron rod to slacken to a greater will,
pummeled on the blackened anvil,
hammer-head thinning the edges, then dropped
fiery into the mold, where one last rough
punch forms the head and it breaks free, the hiss
of water scorching and cooling, one iron nail.

And still the boulders yowl,
enchanted sentinels, sharp-edged and solid,
shadowing the creep of the ocean
up the sand to their feet, over their bulk;
this constancy of water, expanding, retreating,
tumbling over lesser rocks and stones,
specks and contortions,
wearing them down to their smallest intention
like a woman polishing a mirror.

THE WOMAN AT 85

wears her green rubber hip-waders into the calm lake,
casts a nylon line out across
the mist of mosquitoes,
lead sinker hobbling the hook down
with its nightcrawler bait.

A blue boat glides toward her from the far shore,
the woman at the oars a young stranger.
When the large black bass jerks the old woman's hook
she slides off-balance but
the boat woman reaches out to steady her
and the old woman scoops the prickly fish into her net.

The woman at 85 wakes surrounded
by three pictures of Jesus in rainbow robes
and five generations of family framed on her wall,
relieved she won't have to clean the fish, feeling
the woman's hand still warm on her shoulder,
suspended
in the almost celestial quiet before dawn.

FEEDING THE FIRE

Funny how it can start so simply:
a pile of broken sticks, a few crushed
newspapers filled with old stories, ancient
passions; branches from the two of you
parallel-placed with ample breathing
spaces between; then the spark.
Suddenly there is fire leaping against
the soot-dark bricks behind and you are pulled
into the clear eye of the flames roaring,
yellow-orange tongues licking the logs, crackling
into a red center, coals created
warming you both. The secret: never
leave this fire unattended, thinking
it will endure on its own.
Pay attention: it must be fed
as the spirit is fed, vigilantly,
turning a stout branch so the flames will
catch the far side, adding a log
as the rest are broken down; the paradox
that both of you must become a part of
the consuming yet be part of the nurturing;
love as process, keeping the flames
burning steadfastly between you.

BIG CITY WOMAN

came late to wheels
always drives in fourth gear
the radio blares
she plays a keyboard solo
with both hands on the dashboard
carries on philosophical conversations
while scattering ashes
from the lit cigarette
she never smokes

her passengers belt themselves in
ignore the blasting horns

RIDING THE LAKESHORE LIMITED 3:30 AM DECEMBER 22

People's lives flash before my eyes
people I have never known, the lights
in their homes a sudden revelation
Christmas trees already blazing red
and green and white twinkling bursts
porch bulbs illuminating doors,
gas tanks, construction sites, empty roads
the line of street lamps their own map,
equidistant star clusters, a constellation
of highways always moving away, the trees
only rough tumblings of a deeper color
against the night sky blanketed with clouds
hulking low buildings which might be
factories or warehouses and the yellow
halogen lamps pulsing, a neon bar framed
by a yawning parking lot, but
no people anywhere out there, only the ones
restlessly settling in from our last
stop in Rochester, complaining about
their seats, adjusting luggage, children,
bags of gifts. We hurdle forward into
the darkness together, our stories
overlapping for just this small flash of time.

TO MY FATHER WHO WONDERS
OF WHAT PRACTICAL USE IS POETRY

i. Recipe for Poetry Pate`

Mix generously: five pounds shredded poems
preferably of the mixed-metaphor, illegal-rhyme
schools; add romance to taste, a sprinkling of humor.
Serve on melba toast. No calories in the first
helping but thereafter causes gluttonous behavior.

ii. Fireplace Logs

Roll tightly into thick logs: rejection slips,
forgotten poems, old notes written on napkins,
toilet paper, brown bags, envelopes.
Dip in paraffin. Fire carefully. Images rise
in smoke, the bright flames warm the cold watcher,
light the dark room if only for a brief time.

iii. Poet Soup

Boil the bones down, steaming. The air will heave
with a scent of sweat. Fat floats, meat releases
from muscle. Vegetables blur into obscurity,
the pulp a mash of carrots into onions into celery
into beans. To this stock, add the parings of poems:
peels, seeds, veins. Cook until words bubble up,
until the house fills with the heavy smell
and your stomach feels like a cavern
that can never be filled.

ADVICE TO MY NIECE AT HER BIRTH

You will explore, hand over hand,
this world, pushing the limits
far beyond wall, house, yard.
You will jump feet first
into puddles, delighting in
the splash; a rainbow of
droplets clinging to your hair.

Remember this courage, exploration,
blind faith that your feet will hold you.
Wrap it up like a smooth
pebble from the shore,
enclose it as a precious keepsake.

There are those who will tell you,
Be Cautious, Don't Trust, Stay Safe,
who would make you
doubt the strength you feel
in your own legs.

I tell you
the world is dangerous
for those who see danger while
they enclose themselves in iron cages.
The world is sorrow for those
who cling to tears.

Unwrap your pebble, child,
hold it tight and take the plunge,
jump feet first into joy.

REVELATION

The questions of childhood are rising up
like a horde of locusts, like a plague of bats.
They get caught in my window screens,
clog up the chimney swarm across
the walls like a coat of moving paint.
They creep into the deep/down/dark places
looking for food, eat away layer after layer
of myth and lies and commandments and sin
until a new thing arises:

clean as polished bone
sharp as the edge of paper
hard and fine as a crystal goblet;
God, whole as the ocean is whole
moving and churning within a deep bowl of earth.

CREATION I

I came from rock, but before the rock
    there was green:
        energy pushing outward;
            long ribbons intertwined
                reaching for golden sky.

Before the green
    there was water:
        an unceasing dance
            swirls of blue
                cascading down one another.

Before the water
    there was ice:
        silent sheets
            translucent diamonds
                hard with death.

Before the ice
    there was flame:
        orange and yellow and red
            molding, cracking
                strengthening, testing.

Before the flame
    there was wind:
        rushing through space
            long corridors of time
                backwards to the void.

I came from rock but I hold all these within me.
The rock can be broken and out of it will come:
the growing forward,
the dance of rivers,
the crushing of ice,

the flames that in burning, transform;
the breath of wind.
The opening
of that which is hard to soft,
that which is form to fluid,
that which is frozen to energy.

The opening of passion from rock.

ODE TO THE BROKEN TOE

Oh twisted one
oh bone of my bone
so small as to be forgotten
attracting the edges of furniture
chair rungs, table legs
oh great nerve connected
to ground me to my body by
setting me off-balance
with tender pain
with sharp observance
setting me on the right path
oh swollen one
righteous spiritual warrior
you remind me
to feel pain is to reach into being human
to walk is a privilege
to slow down is a gift.   All Praise.

I CAN'T HELP MYSELF

cruising down 95 through the bridge
construction outside New Haven, truck headlights
searing the rear view mirror, 10 mph over
the speed limit on the Garden State Parkway
with this stupid grin on my face, through the tollbooths
that eat coins while I wait for the light
to change from red to green (do not pass the
tollbooths, do not get to you), through
the reststops with a toilet flushing
automatically when I stand up, and faucets
that turn on even when I'm only brushing my hair,
through measured gulps of caffeine, the cold air
shooting through the open sunroof like a shower
keeping my eyes open to the star-points overhead,
through the tattooed man thundering his workboot
against my table at Burger King yelling at me that
I'm working too hard as I write furiously, through
the almost deserted Pennsylvania Turnpike at 2 am,
I steer the VW and try hard to keep from
laughing out loud at the absurdity of this love,
going south to be with you.

SEARCHING FOR A METAPHOR THAT WILL
NOT FRIGHTEN YOU AWAY FROM ME

I do not belong anywhere but
in your heart, your love is my country;
no land holds me
but the land that is your body,
your contours my only typography
of what home could mean,
your beardless face scratchy beneath my hands
the shape of your mouth
like a cave opening.
When you say my name,
an indoor garden spills from your mouth
with lush-sounding plants I used to tend:
angel-wing begonia, coleus, wandering jew,
philodendron, swedish ivy all spreading
green across your landscape.
From your touch rainbows
wrap me up, surround me
with fire and ice,
thunderstorms,
the long sparks of a fire shooting upward.

You are not my world but
the only land I want
and when I go sailing away
I take you with me.
You are solid
but what I love about you
is not solid but lives in
the forest of your eyes
flecked brown and green.

I lay my claim tentatively,
fearful of exile,
your soul so large it fills the sky,
your passion so immense
the sun is jealous.

You bring me mountains to climb,
a slice of agate swirled with blue-green,
the full moon.
I bring you hawthorn vines
twisted into wreaths,
berries blood-red with poison.
I bring you passion scratched out with ink
to show how deeply the roots might grow
if I could let them loose within your land.

AFTER, WHEN YOU ASK WHAT IT'S LIKE

Like the sumptuous magnolia blossoms
scent weighty in the air, their delicate cream
veined with pink rising like cups
to the rain-laden clouds above

Like the great dark angels of cormorants
their wings held crucified by the wind
so black they are holes
in the seascape,
no ink will penetrate their forms

Like the sharp edge of scissors cleanly
slicing thick blue velvet, the velvet
blanketing volcanic rock, the rock
gulping the slate green ocean, the ocean
engulfing scissors, soaking velvet,
rubbing rock down to its core

Like the sound of
the shoreline after a storm
when the heavy waves withdraw
scittering, scratching the stones
back into the rough sea
as if they are stars
being pulled deep into blue velvet.

UPON BEING TOLD MY EXPECTIONS OF
HEAVEN NEED TO BE RAISED

I hone heaven down to its smallest moments,
the here and now, holding them in my heart
until the next one appears:
a baby's wide gaze at the grocery store
her new-tooth grin a glimmer of the beyond;
finding a small rock in the shape of a bear
its steady spirit cool in my hand;
a slight breeze whispering through
the crane's gray feathers
where one moment before there appeared
to be only hewn wood and dead leaves.

These small miracles prepare the way
for heaven's larger revelation:
one maple tree flaming midst the darker pines,
sunlight glinting off the pond
like a million dancing angels,
and you, settled next to me on the log,
carefully eating yogurt, speaking of
your desire to make love to my laugh.

WE ARE BORN AGAIN

Like some Jesus-calling, loose-jawed preacher
or a red-bearded roadshow psychic who sees
the lack of magic in our lives, he reaches down
with his large hands into our throats, through
our lungs, our diaphragms, our legs, our toes,
through our toes and down further yet,
through the floorboards into the earth
and pulls up the sound. A diviner discovering
water under broad layers of dirt and rock with
his forked willow branch, he delights
in drawing the power back up through us
and out into the charged air. And as he's
pulling, directing, softening, strengthening the sound,
we are awestruck with the electricity of it, little kids
again at our first night-time carnival, the lights shining;
our first ride on the Ferris wheel, the wind
in our ears, up, around and down in a wide swoop.
More than that, the first step we take,
the first time we recognize our bodies as beautiful,
ourselves as capable and always being capable.
Or the first time we make love, the sensations
burning into our memories, the pleasure pouring forth,
as this sound transforms us. Some of us want to
weep who never touched this power before, others
rejoice at finding it again, some it scares. But we
can't go away without the power singing in our ears,
tingling in our fingertips, burning into our souls.
Like junkies or the born-again, we return wanting more,
one more fix of the sound power moving through us,
unable yet to harness it ourselves. One more
time when the differences, the connections between
strangers become interdependent, once more
we let the power sing out of us and feel
as if we can change the world with sound.

IT COMES AGAIN

Earth is waking under the snow—
I can smell the drip and dross of melting,
the softening of stark lines of trees,
quickening of air. My husband shovels
the sidewalk of white fluff. Words
come back to me, like a flash
of pure water seen from the highway, far-off;
like a well-traveled path taking
its shape again after the thaw. Language
has been my salvation, the naming of experience,
like a bandage coming off at last to reveal
a puckered scar healing, healing,
as spring makes its way through my hand.

WILL YOU UNDERSTAND
IN MY FIFTIETH YEAR

I find hair to be extraneous, a weight,
a distraction, a flag. I want to
burn myself down to the beginning again,
to a fine ash, create myself anew
with spit and stardust--like being born again,
pushing out the hairless head, everything new
and full of wonder, fresh without context.
I want to build myself atom by swirling atom,
cell by cell, organ by organ, muscle by muscle,
into the spiritual paradox that lives deep within.

I will burn myself down to pure energy
radiating, releasing my photons,
my morphic field encompassing the stars
so that when my body itself is worn down
and becomes extraneous, this essence
of pure energy, this great bird
of my soul will rise up at last
free and soaring, to return home.

ANOTHER POET'S BIO

I am a millipede, motion
my miracle, not numbers;
each leg reaching for a distant
stone to overturn, a blade
of grass to caress, a thick
boot to conquer.

I am a long-barked cypress
skinning myself, doing a slow
strip tease, bark my bustier,
whispering *touch me, sweet stranger,*
pull this roughness from me,
trembling at the grackle's approach.

I am a quick flitting small
rainbowed magic flashing
sleight of the eye and hand
hummingbird in the geraniums,
the petunias, hovering over
the Buddha's bowed head.

This first full length collection of Nita Penfold's work spans 25 years of writing and publishing poetry with over 400 of her poems and several short stories published. In 2005, she received first place in the Judith Siegel Pearson Award from Wayne State University for her poem, "Stigmata."

Pudding House Publications published two chapbooks of her poetry, *The Woman With the Wild-Grown Hair* in 1998 and *Mille-High Blue-Sky Pie* in 2002 and *Hunger Enough: Living Spiritually in a Consumer Society* which she edited for them. (www.puddinghouse.com)

Her poetry has also appeared in the anthologies: *Bless This Child* (Skinner House, 2006), *For All That Is Our Life* (Skinner House, 2005), *House Blessings* (Cotner Books, 2004), *Woman Prayers* (Broadway Books, 2003), *Wedding Blessings* (Andrew McMeel Publishing, 2002), *Fresh Water* (Pudding House Publications, 2002), *Sacred Voices* (HarperSanFrancisco, 2002), *Mothers and Daughters* (Harmony Books, 2001), *Split Verse* (Midmarch Arts Press, 2000), *Family Celebrations* (Andrew McMeel Publishing, 1999), *Prayers to Protest: Poems That Center and Bless Us* (Pudding House Publications, 1998), *Claiming the Spirit Within* (Beacon Press, 1996), *Our Mothers, Our Selves* (Greenwood Publishing Group, 1996), *The Unitarian Universalist Poets* (Pudding House Press, 1996), *Writing Our Way Out Of The Dark* (Queen of Swords Press, 1995), *Women and Death* (Ground Torpedo Press, 1994), *Breaking Up Is Hard To Do* (Crossing Press, 1994), *Love's Shadow* (Crossing Press, 1993), *Fine China: 20 Years of Earth's Daughters* (Springhouse Editions,

1993), If I Had My Life To Live Over, I Would Pick More Daisies (Papier Mache Press, 1992), Catholic Girls, (Plume\Penguin, 1992), Cries Of The Spirit (Beacon Press, 1990), and in these magazines: The New Yorker (Talk of the Town, July 10, 2000), The Maryland Poetry Review, Art Centering, Mother's Underground Magazine, Poetry Motel, Black Buzzard Review, Pudding Magazine, Earth's Daughters, Pacific Coast Journal, Exit 13, The Haven New Poetry (one poet issue, 1987), tenzone, Kumquat Meringue, Slipstream, Moving Out, Sojourner, Bay Windows, among others.

Her fiction has been published in Windchill: Crime Stories by New England Writers (Level Best Books, 2005), Lactuca, Earth's Daughters, Pure Light, The Womansleuth Anthology: Contemporary Mystery Stories By Women (Crossing Press, 1988), and How To: Short-Short Stories by Women (Violet Ink Press, 1993).

She has taught writing workshops at Andover Newton Theological School, Star Island, and Ferry Beach, also through the Outreach and Alternative Education Program at Lesley University and through grants from the Massachusetts Cultural Council and the Milton MA Library. She currently teaches spirituality and arts classes and is adjunct faculty at Andover Newton Theological School.

See **www.nitapenfold.com** for information on other books and workshops.